Speaking through A. Hall

Brian Hickey

WestBow Press
A Division of Thomas Nelson & Zondervan
1663 Liberty Drive
Bloomington, IN 47403
www.westbowpress.com
844-714-3454

ISBN: 978-1-6642-5772-6 (sc)
ISBN: 978-1-6642-5773-3 (e)

Library of Congress Control Number: 2022902871

WestBow Press rev. date: 04/21/2022

WESTBOW
PRESS®
A DIVISION OF THOMAS NELSON
& ZONDERVAN

Contents

HEAVENLY FATHER,
Thank you for all the blessings
Bless the hearts and the changes of hearts that many occur
Allow your will to be done in every aspect
May your word continue to nurture and satisfy thirst
May your word continue to feel us protecting
hands keeping troubles away
And may you continue to lead us to our prepared place

"AMEN"

I.

Even when you had fell
Godsent for you
He has paid for it all
So you have no clue
The troubles you face are that of few
So hold on to JEHOVAH as you go through

"GRABBING GOD"

II.

God shifted you
and then he lifted you, as they said miftsion you
God save gifts to you
Do not worry about closure because what's in store
your access has been granted an opening door

"ALLOWED"

III.

The fire which sets within you burns
The geats of your life turns before speaking
you've learned and in God you have great concern

"THOUGHTFUL"

IV.

To the end is the fight
Don't worry what's wrong
try and make it right
Don't be down as expected
Get up and take flight
If you are going by faith
You won't need sight of the journey you are on
and believe in God with all your might

"FOCUSED"

V.

You thought you didn't have enough
but they you have favor
You were thinking you were all alone
but you have neighbors
When all else is bland
you add flavor
how could you be condemned
when God is your savior

"After All"

VI.

When no one else would
God helped
God stayed as everyone left
At times of danger God protected
No harm to your manger God selected
A God siren shield overall
you love
in Jesus name
We plee the Blood

"Blood Work"

VII.

When the wind is strong
hold on
If someone has gone
hold on
when life does you wrong
hold on
And until Jesus comes back
Stay strong
Hold on

"Hold On"

VIII.

When you came to the end, you made it to a beginning as your frown went away then you start grinning. As life goes by, sometimes you are spinning. Don't worry about the rumors of losing because right now you are winning!

"Hear No Evil"

IX.

You wasn't chosen, you were selected
You weren't being followed
You were being protected
Where God place you
You won't be ejected
And the blessings God has is already perfected

"The Recipient"

X.

A few words and more work
Inside of you God dwell
Outside of you is not well
Not planning will help you fail
Plenty planning will help you prevail

"Blessed"

XI.

I believe with my heart
So in my heart is God
Never shall HE leave
Never will we part
Faithfully I walk to the light
Through the dark
If you can see
Walk as I walk
Go ahead and just start

"Destiny"

XII.

When we can't count
We count on you
At every amount you always come through
As we receive our blessings
Each one comes from you
With GRACE and MERCY
Each day is new
And thank you God and all the Glory is unto you

"Honoring"

XIII.

Siting on the bed but not alone
I can hear someone speaking
But without a tone
The presence feels familiar
But the body is gone
I wonder did they come back so that I would feel strong

"Company"

XIV.

I was given salvation
In a time of restoration
With on hesitation
God had beautified the presentation
In the eyes of a visualizing nation
So receive God's stabilization
During and after your creation
There will be an elevation that speaks of you and God's relation

"Never Forsaken"

XV.

Sisters are God's gift
This is not a rumor nor is it a mift
A lot of times what they do we see
Other times they do what be
A God given spirit with mighty strength
that will help you fight
Battles at any length
A humble person that do as they do
And with a love that's so honest and true

"A Beautiful Bond"

XVI.

You can not see light that doesn't shine
Even though there is a light that shines all the time
You cannot hear sounds that are not heard
But one of the mouth that God so spoken–is the word
You will not sow a seed
If there is no land
So the seed is gathered inside of your hand
So give unto God what is right
And blessed will be both your days and nights

"Sowing"

XVII.

God blessed the grandmother that is great
One thing that makes you great is your faith
What blesses your faith is God's GRACE
Grace is granted while seeking God's FACE!

"Looking"

XVIII.

Noone else came, but that's ok
When Jesus was called
He was on the way
Noone else seen nor heard a tear
But as you cry God catches your tears
If you think someone is close and you do not want to part
That's ok because God is in your heart

"Inseparable"

XIX.

In spite of how you are treated, you live
In spite of what is taken, you give
God is ordering you, so you will walk right
And he gives you the words so you will speak inspite

"Inspite"

XX.

God sent me so I came
He asked me to speak HIS name
And as I speak
To not be ashamed
But if I fall
Place no blame
And my brother always claim
Even when he receives his fame
And when I do "ME"
God will claim!

"Ownership"

XXI.

You didn't catch it
because there was nothing tossed
You couldn't find me
because I was never lost
You can't fire me
Because you are not my boss
And you won't hang me
Because you won't pick up my cross

"Can Not and Will Not"

As things start to fall
Others begin to rise
It is all a test of faith
Continue to try
Try not to worry
Try to be encouraged
Try to go on
In faith that's strong

"Please Hold On!"

Printed in the United States
by Baker & Taylor Publisher Services